AF561723
I AM HELPFUL
A Coloring Book For Girls & Boys

Published By: SketchBuddies®

ISBN: 978-81-941108-4-2

Hey... Thank You for being AWESOME!

We hope that you have a fun time with your book. We have a gift for you. You can download a free printable set of our best coloring pages by visiting our website : SketchBuddies.com

It would be so cool if you could share your completed images with us. You can find us on / @vrSketchBuddies & on @vr_SketchBuddies.

We are always working hard to improve our books. Please let us know how we are doing by writing a review of our book on your favorite online book store.
You can always reach out to us on social media. #vrSketchBuddies

My name is ______________

Stick Your
Picture Here

My Superpower is
I like to Help others
I Am Helpful
H

I like being
HELPFUL

Helping others
makes me feel Good

I pick up my toys
after playing with them

I ♥ MOM
I help to change and fold the laundry
5

I help to put dirty clothes in the hamper
5

I help to
set the table

I help to put dirty dishes in the sink

I
keep my
bedroom
clean

I help
to take out
the trash

I help to
make the dinner
FLOUR

I help to
carry the
groceries

I do my best
in finishing my
household chores

I handle
all my
responsibilities
and tasks well

I love to help others.
It makes me feel good.

Whatever I do
I give my best

Everyone Loves Me
because I am Helpful

I help others
because
I am strong and
responsible person

I Help Others
because
It makes Me HAPPY

I Help my teacher in the classroom
2
7
8
1
6
0
4
B
A
C
9
3
jazz
jazz

I always Help
my Friends
when they need me

I Like to Help
when someone asks me

I Help People
who are sad
by making them
feel good

I know that
it is okay to
ask for Help

I am not afraid
to ask for Help
when I need it

When other people
need me,
I am there to
Help them

I AM HELPFUL

jazz
jazz
Being
Helpful
is
COOL

What did you do to help today?
jazz
jazz

www.ingramcontent.com/pod-product-compliance
Lightning Source LLC
LaVergne TN
LVHW070400230826
846093LV00017B/549
* 9 7 8 8 1 9 4 1 1 0 8 4 2 *